D0990733

# CHARLES EAMES

## FURNITURE
## FROM THE DESIGN COLLECTION
THE MUSEUM OF MODERN ART, NEW YORK
BY ARTHUR DREXLER

## DEPARTMENT OF ARCHITECTURE & DESIGN

Arthur Drexler, *Director*
Emilio Ambasz, *Curator of Design*
John Garrigan, *Assistant Curator of Graphic Design*
Mary Jane Lightbown, *Research Associate*
Kathryn Eno, *Assistant to the Director*
Katherine Mansfield, *Secretary*
Jerry Bowen, *Custodian*

Ludwig Glaeser, *Curator of the Mies van der Rohe Archive*
Susan Evens, *Secretary*
Carol Sullivan, *Cataloguer*
Anny Eder, *Conservator*
Margarete Hachigian, *Researcher*

## COMMITTEE ON ARCHITECTURE & DESIGN

Philip Johnson, *Chairman*
Mrs. Douglas Auchincloss
Armand P. Bartos
Ivan Chermayeff
Arthur Drexler
Mrs. Richard Duffalo
Jack Lenor Larsen
Mrs. Charles P. Noyes
Donald Page
T. Merrill Prentice, Jr.

Dabney Lancaster Library
Longwood College
Farmville, Virginia

| | |
|---|---|
| NK<br>2439<br>.E2<br>D73<br><br>749.2 E12f | Eames, Charles.<br><br>Furniture from the<br>design collection,<br>the Museum of Modern<br>Art, New York |

## TRUSTEES OF THE MUSEUM OF MODERN ART

William S. Paley, *Chairman*
Gardner Cowles, *Vice Chairman*
Henry Allen Moe, *Vice Chairman*
David Rockefeller, *Vice Chairman*
Mrs. John D. Rockefeller 3rd, *President*
J. Frederic Byers III, *Vice President*
Mrs. Bliss Parkinson, *Vice President*
James Thrall Soby, *Vice President*
Neal J. Farrell, *Treasurer*
Robert O. Anderson
Mrs. Douglas Auchincloss
Walter Bareiss
Robert R. Barker
Alfred H. Barr, Jr.*
Mrs. Armand P. Bartos
William A. M. Burden
Ivan Chermayeff
Mrs. Kenneth B. Clark
John de Menil
Mrs. C. Douglas Dillon
Williiam H. Donaldson
Mrs. Edsel B. Ford*
Gianluigi Gabetti
George Heard Hamilton
Wallace K. Harrison*
Mrs. Walter Hochschild*
James W. Husted*
Philip Johnson
Mrs. Frank Y. Larkin
Gustave L. Levy
John L. Loeb
Ranald H. Macdonald*
Mrs. G. Macculloch Miller*
J. Irwin Miller
Richard E. Oldenburg
Mrs. Charles S. Payson*
Gifford Phillips
Nelson A. Rockefeller
Mrs. Wolfgang Schoenborn
Mrs. Bertram Smith
Mrs. Alfred R. Stern
Mrs. Donald B. Straus
Walter N. Thayer
Edward M. M. Warburg*
Clifton R. Wharton, Jr.
Monroe Wheeler*
John Hay Whitney

*\*Honorary Trustee for Life*

Copyright © 1973. Printed in the U.S.A.
The Museum of Modern Art, 11 West 53rd Street,
New York 10019
Library of Congress Catalogue Card Number 73-76672
ISBN 0-87070-314-5

Second Printing

# INTRODUCTION

This survey of furniture by Charles Eames is the first in a series devoted to important groups of material in the Design Collection of the Museum of Modern Art.

The most original American furniture designer since Duncan Phyfe, Charles Eames has contributed at least three of the major chair designs of the twentieth century. He has also given a personal and pervasive image to the idea of lightness and mobility. His work has influenced furniture design in virtually every country, and his mastery of advanced technology has set new standards of both design and production. The first of his chairs, executed in collaboration with the architect Eero Saarinen (1910-1961) emerged from a 1940 Museum of Modern Art competition. Since then furniture by Eames has been mass-produced in quantities that must now be counted by the millions, and more than 50 examples of his work have entered the Museum's Design Collection.

Concerned primarily with mass-produced useful objects made to serve a specific purpose, the Design Collection was formally inaugurated in 1934 with objects culled from the "Machine Art" exhibition organized by Philip Johnson. Since then the Collection has grown to more than 2,100 examples, representing all the arts of manufacture, and classified within the following categories: appliances and equipment; furniture; tableware; tools; and textiles. In size and diversity they range from such mass-produced artifacts as pill boxes, typewriters and radios to chairs and tables, an automobile, and even such semi-architectural productions as the entrance arch to a Paris Métro Station.

Two criteria apply in the selection of objects: *quality* and *historical significance*.

An object is chosen for its quality because it is thought to achieve, or to have originated, those formal ideals of beauty which have become the major style concepts of our time.

Historical significance is a more flexible criterion. It applies to objects which may not resolve problems of aesthetics and function with total success, but which nevertheless have contributed importantly—or may yet contribute—to the development of design.

Reflecting these separate but related considerations, the Design Collection is administered in two sections. Objects thought to be of such excellence that, even if not major works of their kind, they may still be said to have secured their place in the history of design, are incorporated in the Collection as "permanent" acquisitions. Material of supplementary and perhaps less certain interest is accessioned into the Study Collection. Both categories are continuously reviewed, and as critical judgment changes material is occasionally shifted from one to the other. Study Collection material may be de-accessioned at the discretion of the Department of Architecture and Design and its advisory Trustee Committee; material in the Design Collection proper may be accessioned and de-accessioned only with the approval of the Museum's Board of Trustees.

About 200 objects illustrating the history of modern design and its relevant nineteenth century forebears may be seen in the Museum's Goodwin Galleries. Much of the material in this exhibition is changed from time to time, but certain key works are almost always on view.

Arthur Drexler, *Director*
*Department of Architecture and Design*

78— 8278

**1**

**1** Furniture by Charles Eames and Eero Saarinen, Museum of Modern Art's "Organic Design in Home Furnishings" exhibition, 1941.

**2** Scale models by Eames and Saarinen.

**2**

It is difficult now to recall the fervor with which early champions of modern architecture fought to change our buildings and the artifacts that fill them. By the mid-1930s Marcel Breuer and Ludwig Mies van der Rohe in Germany, and Le Corbusier in France, had established what seemed to be prototypical solutions for most design problems. Particularly in furniture, German and French work seemed emblematic of the modern spirit: its talismans were precise, machined (or handcrafted to look machined), and apparently useful. Where the Germans and French worked with metal, Finland's Alvar Aalto preferred wood; this was understood as a wholesome Scandinavian taste for nature, and perhaps also a certain slackness in responding to the dictates of function.

With the arrival at Harvard of Walter Gropius in 1937, and Mies van der Rohe at the Armour Institute of Technology in 1938, the ideals and methods of German functionalism were rapidly adapted to the American scene. But public acceptance of Bauhaus principles lagged; young architects emerging from Harvard could more readily persuade their clients to accept a modernism of Scandinavian rather than German character, and it was Aalto's furniture that was first to appear in small specialty stores. Most modern furniture was costly, and none of it was widely available.

In this context the Museum of Modern Art responded enthusiastically to a suggestion made by Bloomingdale's department store in New York City. Bloomingdale's, recognizing the emergence of a younger generation open to new design ideas, wanted to find designers who could produce work of good quality. Toward this end the Museum conducted in 1940 an inter-American competition for the design of home furnishings. Other stores, and eventually manufacturers, also joined in sponsoring the project, which was called "Organic Design in Home Furnishings".

Exhibitions involving ideas of the moment are always difficult to title, and usually end up tagged with a phrase either too narrowly specific or too ambiguously vague. The term "organic" was explained in the exhibition catalog by Eliot Noyes, the Director of the Museum's Department of Industrial Design, who had recently completed his studies with Gropius at Harvard. "A design may be called organic", Noyes wrote, "when there is an harmonious organization of the parts within the whole, according to structure, material, and purpose. Within this definition there can be no vain ornamentation or superfluity, but the part of beauty is none the less great–in ideal choice of material, in visual refinement, and in the rational elegance of things intended for use".

As Noyes now observes, this definition of organic was not altogether persuasive. It seeks to relate ideas that have no necessary conjunction: thus utility emerges as the ultimate determinant of form; and beauty is a by-product of "rational" decisions. The exhibition catalog reviews the pioneering work of several modern designers but omits any mention of Frank Lloyd Wright, who popularized the term. Yet Wright's understanding of it would have emphasized "wholeness". Like Aristotle, who first defined it, he would have understood a "whole" as something in which the position and shape of the parts in relation to each other make a difference more consequential than "harmony". The genuine part of a whole cannot retain its own character except in the whole of which it is a part. To remove it is to destroy the part and mutilate the whole.

This conception derives from the example of living organisms; and it is not surprising that in popular usage "organic design" means forms and materials found in nature, prevalently curvilinear, and frequently embodying the marks of their own history and "growth" under the craftsman's hand. (Characteristics, incidentally, of much Scandinavian design until the 'sixties). But in the philosophy of

OVERLEAF

**3-10** COMPETITION DRAWINGS.
Eames and Saarinen.
"Organic Design in Home Furnishings", 1940.
Eight of ten drawings, colored pencil and collage on white poster board. 20″ x 30″.

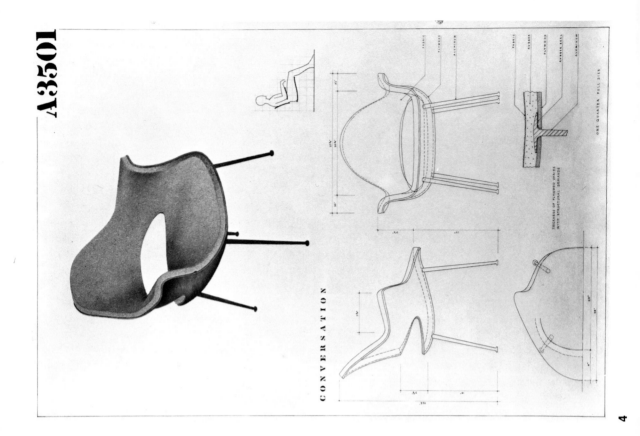

## A3501

CONVERSATION

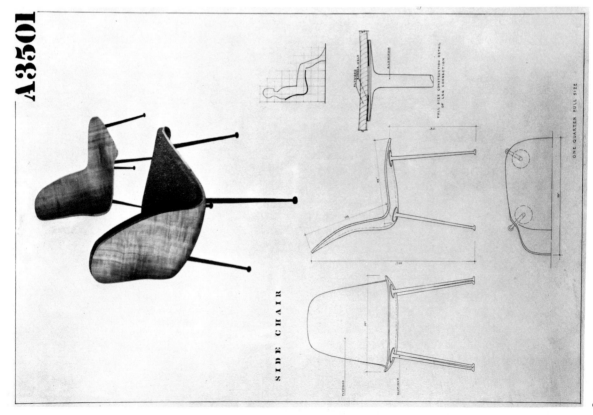

## A3501

SIDE CHAIR

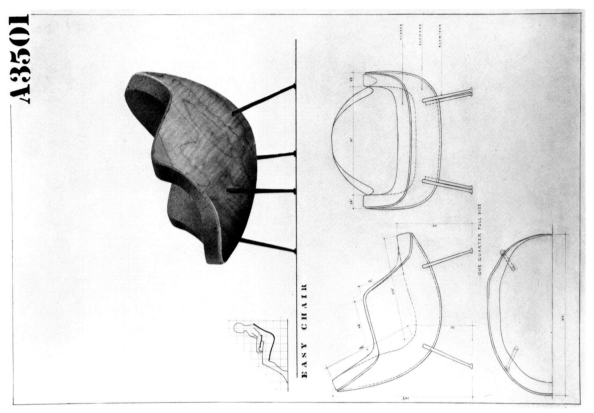

EASY CHAIR

ONE QUARTER FULL SIZE

A3501

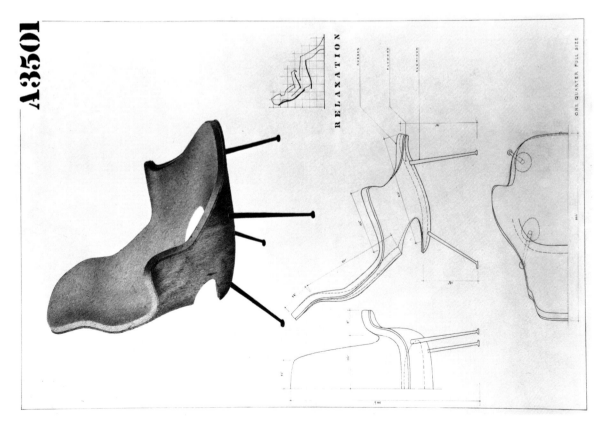

RELAXATION

ONE QUARTER FULL SIZE

A3501

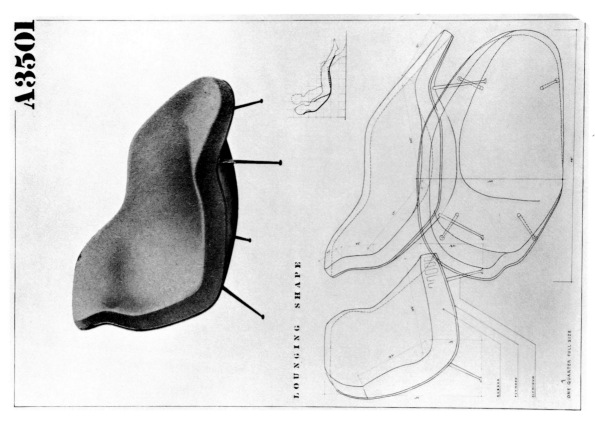

A3501

LOUNGING SHAPE

ONE QUARTER FULL SIZE

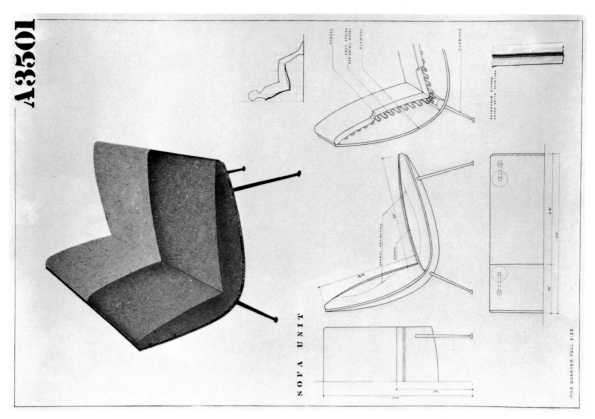

A3501

SOFA UNIT

ONE QUARTER FULL SIZE

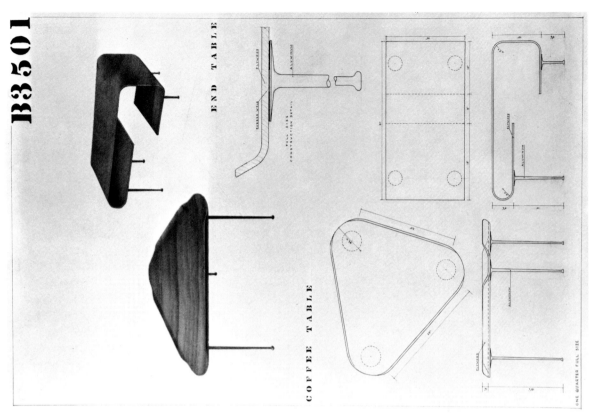

B3501

END TABLE

COFFEE TABLE

FULL SIZE CONSTRUCTION DETAIL

ONE QUARTER FULL SIZE

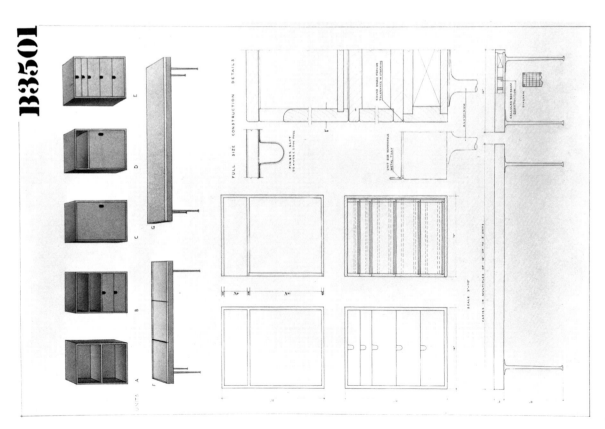

B3501

FULL SIZE CONSTRUCTION DETAILS

SCALE 3"=1'0"

CASES IN MULTIPLES OF 18" OR 24" TO 3 UNITS

**11**

**12**

aesthetics the primary meaning of "organic" refers to a kind of wholeness different from harmony and other forms of aggregation, because it precludes the possibility of interchangeable parts. The point is of some interest because, when the results of the competition were published and exhibited in 1941, the designs by Eames and Saarinen combined both "organic" and "aggregate" solutions, and a struggle with this formal problem has marked Eames' work ever since.

First prize for seating and other living room furniture went to the entries jointly submitted by Eero Saarinen and Charles Eames. Both men were at that time associated with the Cranbrook Academy of Art in Michigan, Eero being the son of the School's Director, the architect Eliel Saarinen. Eames, born in St. Louis in 1907, had studied architecture and opened his own architectural office in 1930. In 1936 he accepted a fellowship and later a teaching post at Cranbrook. Besides Eero Saarinen his colleagues there included Florence Knoll, Harry Bertoia, Harry Weese, Ralph Rapson, and Ray Kaiser; all of whom were subsequently to do important work in architecture and design. Ray Kaiser, who had studied painting with Hans Hoffman, assisted Eames and Saarinen in preparing the competition entries.

Of the winning designs from the United States, Mexico, Uruguay, Argentina, and Brazil, most had in common a simplicity of construction due as much to economy as to aesthetic principles. The Eames and Saarinen designs for seating were unique in requiring an important structural innovation. All of their chairs made use of plywood shells, not bent in one direction, as had already been done by Aalto and Breuer, but molded in two directions. The resulting compound curves are emphatically three-dimensional, relating the chairs to sculpture in that they are not completely intelligible when seen in profile but must be seen in the round. Moreover, the double curvature of the molded plywood allows the use of thin veneers laminated to layers of glue, achieving considerable strength.

**13**

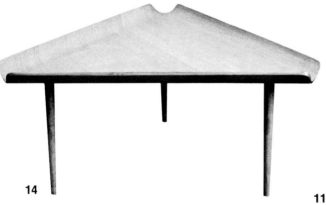

**14**

**11, 12**  Cut-away examples of sectional sofa and lounge chair, showing construction details.

**13**  Storage cabinets on benches, combined with two-legged desk.

**14**  Triangular coffee table with molded plywood top.

In the design for a sectional seating unit (7, 11) the shell supports flat springs which in turn carry layers of padding, foam rubber, and upholstery cloth. The light shell replaces bulkier wood frame construction, but an even greater advance toward lightness and simplicity was achieved with the molded shells for armchairs (4, 5, 12). Here springs have been eliminated and a foam rubber pad alone provides softness.

In four of the chairs the shells are one-piece elements incorporating the arms as well as the seat and back. Only legs are designed as separate elements. By 1941 Chrysler Corporation had developed a process called cycle-welding, whereby wood could be joined to rubber, glass, or metal. Eames had intended to use this technique to connect aluminum legs to the inside surfaces of the molded shells. But the cycle-weld process was reserved for military purposes in World War II, preventing Eames from using it commercially. Instead, the competition designs were finally executed with wood legs, which penetrated the shells and were fastened from within by a metal flange.

Apart from the unavoidable problems of strength and durability imposed by this change of plan, the treatment of legs as thin spikes with no apparent connection to the shell—visually as well as structurally—insists on the formal integrity of the shell as an element whose function does not include supporting itself. Of all the shells, two are of particular interest for their sculptural configurations: those described as being for "relaxation" and for "lounging" (5, 8). The relaxation chair is given a convincing plasticity by its high back, and by the opening which occurs where the back would meet the seat (so that the back is in effect cantilevered from the sides of the shell). The lounging chair owes its interest to its asymmetry, and perhaps to the coy posture it implies. Eames returned to the idea in 1948 (64), but no version has ever been manufactured.

The other entry by Saarinen and Eames comprised a group of cabinets and coffee tables, later supplemented by desk-tables. Like most designers of modern furniture, their solution to the problem of storage called for boxes of uniform dimensions, the interesting innovation being that the boxes were not to support themselves but were to be carried on separate benches, which could also function as seats (9, 10, 13, 14).

Production and distribution of this furniture, like the other winning designs, was severely limited by the war. In 1941 Ray Kaiser and Charles Eames were married and moved to southern California, where they worked to develop low-cost techniques for wood lamination and molding. This research resulted in a commission from the U.S. Navy to produce molded plywood stretchers and splints (16). By 1946 they had designed a new set of molded plywood chairs, which the Museum exhibited in a one-man show and which the Herman Miller Company began to produce, using tools developed in the Eames' Venice workshop.

Of the chairs included in the Museum's 1946 exhibition, the side chair of molded plywood with metal rod legs, produced in both dining and lounge heights, emerged as a completely successful—and beautiful—design (25). Among the many ingenious designs that followed it, the molded plywood and leather-padded lounge chair (68), and perhaps the aluminum frame lounge chair (74) would now also appear to be major achievements in the development of 20th century furniture.

Eero Saarinen, in his own later work, pursued the notion of one-piece, one-material as the ideal formal solution. Eames has played with the idea but finds it dogmatic. The problem, in his own words, began with "How do you hold two wood shells in space?" He has tended to develop sophisticated technical solutions first, and only later re-design the sometimes disparate parts to make them harmonize.

It is characteristic of Eames' furniture that it can be scattered or clustered but need not be formally aligned, affording a flexibility of use that has been much admired by his fellow architects. "I think of myself officially as an architect", Eames has said; "I can't help but look at the problems around us as problems of structure—and structure is architecture".

**15**

**15** Charles Eames (left) and Eero Saarinen in 1941.

**16** LEG SPLINT. 1942.
Molded plywood. 41½″ l.

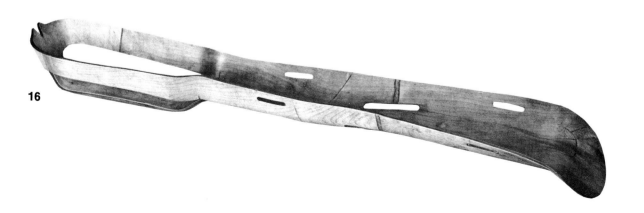

**16**

Significant innovations in chair design and production begin in 1856 with Michael Thonet's process for steaming and bending solid rods of beechwood. Thonet's light, strong chairs were sold through illustrated catalogs and have endured extremes of climate from Alaska to Brazil. The famous example shown here (17) was used by Le Corbusier in many of his buildings, and like some of the more flamboyantly curvilinear Thonet designs is still in production.

The developments which inaugurate modern design rely not on curvilinear embellishment but on the reduction of form and material to their essentials. Ludwig Mies van der Rohe's tubular steel side chair of 1926, the first and still the most elegant of its kind, is really a three dimensional diagram of structure, carrying seat and back elements of leather or cane attached directly to the steel (18).

Marcel Breuer's 1928 side chair combines a steel tube with applied seat and back panels of cane mounted to wood frames. Its modest dimensions and trim lines have made it one of the most popular chairs of the twentieth century (19).

Both the Breuer and Mies chairs replace Thonet's wood rods with steel tubes. The increase in strength allows cantilever construction; supported at the front only, such chairs flex under the weight of their occupants. Alvar Aalto achieved a similar strength and flexibility with bent plywood, in his 1934 lounge chair (20). Here the seat alone flexes; in other designs Aalto made cantilevered plywood frames also strong enough to flex without breaking.

In the chairs by Mies, Breuer and Aalto each part is given its own distinct shape and material. But in 1946 Mies made dozens of sketches of a chair to be made of one material —molded plastic—in one piece. These sketches inspired the entry by Robert Lewis and James Prestini to the Museum of Modern Art's 1948 Low-cost Furniture Competition (21). Materials and techniques were still too costly, and it seemed unlikely that the public would accept an unupholstered lounge chair. The idea of a chair made as a sculptural object in one material, and if possible in one piece, was fitfully pursued. One of the most stylish efforts was Eero Saarinen's 1957 armchair of molded plastic balanced on a stem pedestal. Limitations of strength resulted in the pedestal being made of aluminum, painted white to match the plastic (22).

Not until Verner Panton's 1968 side chair was it possible to mass-produce a truly one-piece chair of plastic which, moreover, reintroduces the cantilever (23). In Italy the idea has been pursued with fervor, but the results are not always distinguished for comfort. Techniques developed in Europe and the United States now make it possible to laminate plastic foam and fabric to plastic shells, thus maintaining the comfort allowed by more conventional construction.

17 GEBRUDER THONET, Austria.
   Armchair. c. 1870. Bent beechwood. 31″ h.

18 LUDWIG MIES VAN DER ROHE
   Side chair. 1926. Chrome-plated steel tube; leather. 30½″ h.

19 MARCEL BREUER
   Side chair. 1928. Chrome-plated steel tube; wood; cane. 32″ h.

20 ALVAR AALTO
   Lounge chair. c. 1934. Bent birch plywood. 25½″ h.

21 ROBERT LEWIS, JAMES PRESTINI
   Lounge chair. 1948. Molded plastic. 34″ h.

22 EERO SAARINEN
   Armchair. 1957. Molded plastic reinforced with Fiberglas; painted aluminum base. 32″ h.

23 VERNER PANTON
   Side chair. 1968. Molded plastic. 32½″ h.

17

18

20

19

22

21

23

By 1946 the techniques for manufacturing molded plywood chairs were developed enough to allow production of more than 5,000 units. Begun in the Eames studio, and later taken over by the Herman Miller Furniture Company, this production concentrated on the side chair with which Eames achieved worldwide renown.

Made in both dining and lounge heights, the design employs ⅝″ diameter steel rods to form both the front and back legs; and a ⁷⁄₁₆″ diameter rod to make the connecting spine which also carries the backrest. Rubber shock mounts bolted to the metal frame and bonded to the wood give the entire chair a comfortable resilience which is part of its strength, belying its apparent fragility (24).

The 5-ply wood panels, molded in compound curves, are ⁵⁄₁₆″ thick. Although now made only in walnut, early production used ash, walnut and birch; one model used birch stained bright red or black. Originally the metal legs were equipped with rubber tips; because they tended to fall off Eames later developed the permanently attached self-leveling nylon glides used in current production.

Part of the elegance of this design must be attributed to the contours of the seat and, even more, the back panel. Eames himself cites the hundreds of studies discarded because the contours of these two elements somehow attracted undue attention. The back panel might be described as a rectangle about to turn into an oval, the transformation being arrested at a point midway between the two shapes. Ambiguous but not bland, the shape is instantly seen as a whole, with no part of its contour catching the eye (27). The curve of the seat flares more emphatically and from certain angles gives the chair a curiously animated look.

The look and the technology can be imitated, although the technology requires rather more effort. During the late 'forties extreme lightness in furniture design and construction came to be associated with a style of deportment epitomizing California and, by implica-

**24, 25** DINING CHAIR. 1946.
Molded walnut plywood; steel rods; rubber shock-mounts. 29½″ h.

**26, 27, 28** DINING CHAIR. 1946.
Molded walnut plywood; steel rods; rubber shock-mounts. 29½″ h.

**26**

**27**

28                                                                29

30

**29, 30**  LOW SIDE CHAIR. 1946.
Molded walnut plywood; steel rods; rubber shockmounts. 27⅜″ h.

31

32

tion, the rest of youthful America, much as carved, oiled, and knobbily jointed wood was thought to proclaim Scandinavian moderation.

The distinctive and memorable image contributed by what is now called simply "the Eames chair" does indeed have about it something that seems American. It does not suppress necessary mechanical details but rather makes them plainly visible. Hardware is pragmatically designed to do a job, but not overdesigned in the romanticizing manner Americans often identify as European. Nevertheless, the Eames approach has its own romantic commitment: it derives from the belief that there is an inherent good in making the greatest use of the least amount of material. It achieves its purpose by separating functions and defining them in the narrowest possible way, so that each will require a specific shape and material; hence the importance of connectors and other items of hardware.

In 1946 the Museum of Modern Art devoted a small exhibition to the metal and wood side chairs and other related work, including some experimental chairs that were never mass-produced. Two of these are simply variations in the arrangement of legs for the dining chair. In one a single leg is placed at the front (34); in the other it is at the back (33). The latter version also uses a doubled length of rod for greater strength. Both versions were discarded because they were not sufficiently stable.

More interesting were the versions designed to be unstable: chairs with a projecting rear leg shorter than the others, so that the restless occupant could tilt back until the rear leg touched the floor (35, 36). Chairs designed to absorb energy, like Greek "worry beads", might have been expected to enjoy a wide market; these, however, were not produced.

31  Eames installation for 1946 Museum of Modern Art exhibition, "New Furniture Designed by Charles Eames".

32  Mies van der Rohe installation of Eames furniture for the Museum's 1947 exhibition, "One Hundred Useful Objects of Fine Design".

**33**

33  SIDE CHAIR. c. 1944.
Molded plywood stained red; single back leg of double steel rod. 29½″ h.

34  SIDE CHAIR. c. 1944.
Molded canaletta plywood; single front leg. 29¾″ h.

**34**

35

36

37

**38**

Among the variations of the lounge and dining height chairs to enter production was a design executed entirely in wood. Few examples reveal Eames' methods and preferences more clearly. Apart from the appeal of wood for those who find metal unpleasant to the touch, the presumed advantage of the all-wood chairs was a greater uniformity of design. A single material is used for both supporting and supported elements. But because the seat and back are molded in compound curves, their strength and rigidity can be provided by conspicuously thin sheets of plywood. The carrying structure, being made of lengths of plywood bent in one plane only, must be considerably thicker. The resulting visual discrepancy contradicts the intended simplification (40).

From Eames' point of view, it was finally preferable to use two different materials— wood and metal—for the two different functions being served, emphasizing the differences rather than trying to minimize them.

Nevertheless, the all-wood chairs remain among the most interesting of Eames' designs. A further variation is the wood chair with padding held in place by a veneer of leather glued along the edges of the seat and back panels (38).

**39**

**38**   LOW SIDE CHAIR. 1946.
Molded and bent birch plywood; laminated leather and padding. 25½″ h.

**39**   LOW SIDE CHAIR. 1946.
Molded and bent birch plywood. 25¾″ h.

**40**   DINING CHAIR. 1946.
Molded and bent birch plywood. 29½″ h.

**41**

**42**

**43**

Eames' experiments in molding plywood continued from 1941 to 1948. The objective was primarily the resolution of technical problems, but aesthetics played an almost equally important part. Eames and his associates seldom work from drawings; preliminary sketches, according to Eames, have consisted mostly of rough notes meant to indicate a general configuration. Designs are worked out at full scale, the compound curves of seat and back elements being developed over closely spaced templates. This method allows frequent tests for comfort, and construction drawings for the metal molds that will later be required for mass production are made from the templates themselves.

Some of these experimental chairs were discarded for functional reasons. The three-legged dining chair, like its metal-legged companions, tipped over too easily (41). Other experiments, though functionally quite satisfactory, were rejected either because the shapes were not pleasing or because they were too numerous and hence too expensive to produce. In this latter category, the armchair (43) and the lounge chair on a tubular metal base (44) can now be seen as important stages in the development of the leather-cushioned armchair discussed on page 41. And even the unpadded plywood chair on its precarious metal perch (45) was subsequently developed in two distinct versions.

**44**

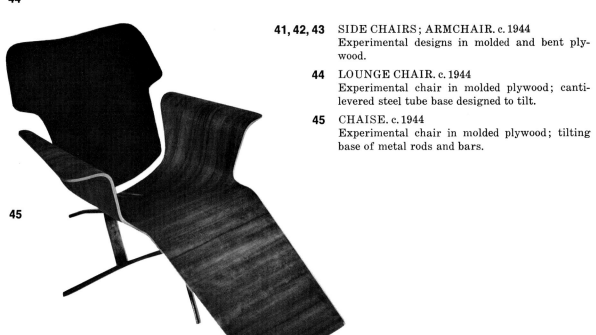

**45**

**41, 42, 43** SIDE CHAIRS; ARMCHAIR. c. 1944
Experimental designs in molded and bent plywood.

**44** LOUNGE CHAIR. c. 1944
Experimental chair in molded plywood; cantilevered steel tube base designed to tilt.

**45** CHAISE. c. 1944
Experimental chair in molded plywood; tilting base of metal rods and bars.

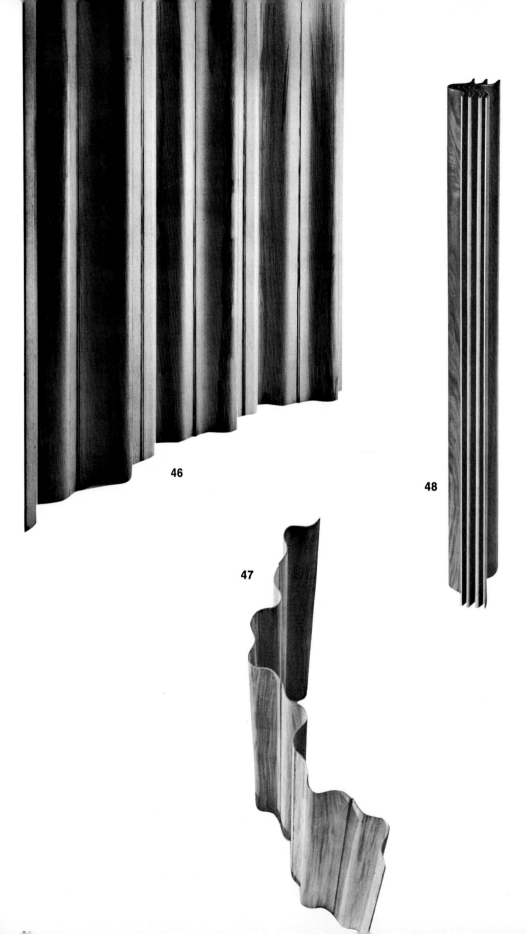

46

48

47

A by-product of Eames' experiments with molded plywood was a simple but ingenious folding screen, made of 34″ or 68″ lengths of plywood. Each piece was pressed into a flattened U curve. The pieces were joined to each other by a full-length canvas hinge, sandwiched into the laminations. Because each section was only 9½″ wide, the screen allowed greater flexibility in its placement than more conventional designs using flat and wider panels. The repeated curves of the fully extended screen formed an undulating wall with the intrinsic interest of an abstract sculpture (47). The canvas hinges were wide enough to allow the sections to fold back and nest in each other, making a narrow package easily stored in a closet (48). Unfortunately, the market proved too small to sustain production and this excellent design was withdrawn.

Of similar elegance, but technically less successful, was a table with folding metal legs (49). A V-shaped brace resembling an opened hairpin formed a hinge connection to the thin legs.

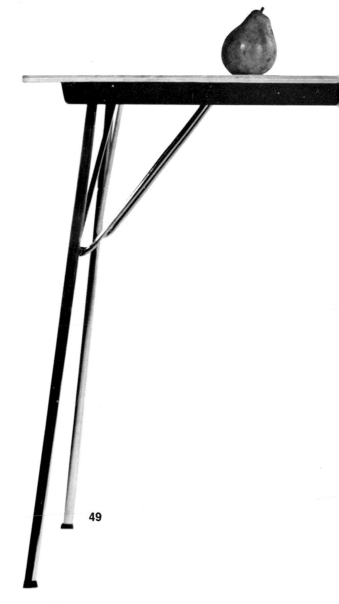

49

Eames was trained as an architect and opened his own office in 1930. He and Eero Saarinen designed a house for John Entenza in 1949; in the same year an adjacent house was designed by Eames for his own use. Both buildings were in the series of Case Study Houses commissioned by Entenza for his magazine "California Arts and Architecture". The Eames house was among the most important buildings of the years following World War II, but architecture soon ceased to be Eames' major interest.

The Eames approach to architecture involved a cheerful acceptance of mass-produced materials. Stock window and door elements, normally used in the construction of factories, were combined with steel columns and open web joists, all ordered from their manufacturers' catalogs (55). Notwithstanding minor modifications made to some of these parts, the house is a collection of ready-mades anticipating "The Whole Earth Catalog", that compendium of engaging and oddly useful products first published in 1968.

Architects and critics hailed Eames' house for demonstrating a kind of pre-fabrication. Filled with transparent and translucent glass, and stucco or metal siding, the delicate steel frames produce an effect of lightness similar to that of a Japanese tea house (56). The interior, crowded with toys, flowers, and furniture, has an air of playfulness not often associated with architecture of industrial origin (57). Eames' emphasis on structural technique accorded well with the emerging influence of Mies van der Rohe's steel and glass buildings in Chicago, to which the house owed some of its clarity. But the direction taken by Mies was toward simplification, and the somber aspect of his structural forms moved architecture away from whatever might seem casual or arbitrary. Mies proceeded by subtraction; Eames by addition; and the promising lead given by the Eames house remains to be explored.

EAMES HOUSE AND STUDIO, Santa Monica, California. 1949.

55   East elevation of house and studio.

56   North elevation, house.

57   Living room; bedrooms on balcony above.

**56**

**57**

**58**

58  LOW ARMCHAIR. 1950.
    Molded polyester; wire; rubber shockmounts.
    23″ h.

59  ARMCHAIR, Rocker. 1950.
    Molded polyester; wire; birch runners; rubber
    shockmounts. 26¾″ h.

60  ARMCHAIR. 1950.
    Molded polyester; metal rod; rubber shockmounts.
    31¼″ h.

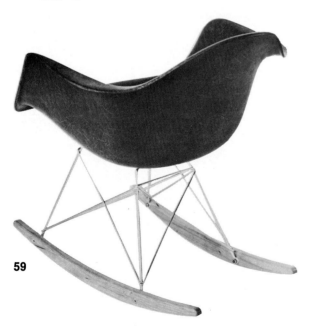

**59**

Eames had been considering the mass production of stamped aluminum or steel furniture when, in 1948, The Museum of Modern Art conducted an "International Competition for Low-cost Furniture Design", directed by Edgar Kaufmann, Jr. "Metal stamping", Eames said in the text accompanying his entry, "is the technique synonymous with mass production in this country, yet 'acceptable' furniture in this material is noticeably absent . . . By using forms that reflect the positive nature of the stamping technique in combination with a surface treatment that cuts down heat transfer, dampens sound, and is pleasant to the touch, we feel it is possible to free metal furniture of the negative bias from which it has suffered". The Eames entry, prepared with a University of California team, shared second prize for seating.

By 1950, when the results of the competition were manufactured, published and exhibited, economical production of molded plastic, rather than metal, had been set up by the Herman Miller Furniture Company. The published designs were of plastic, although the metal versions were actually exhibited. The switch from stamped metal to molded plastic required only minor design modifications—an interesting aside on "the nature of materials" as a significant determinant of form. Conceivably the same shapes could also have been made of papier-maché or concrete; the only visible variation induced by different materials is the thickness of the edge.

Manufactured with legs either of metal rod (60), or a kind of cat's-cradle of metal wire, or wire with wood rockers (58, 59), the chair has been a remarkably serviceable object. Its imitations suffer from the defects of the original: the visual relationship of the shell to any kind of metal base is at best problematic. It is perhaps most convincing in the low lounge (58). A side chair version without arms (62) was also developed as a stacking chair (61) and is a singularly compact and sturdy solution to the problem of storage; the same shape was also made of bent wire with an upholstered pad in fabric or leather, making a somewhat more unified design (63).

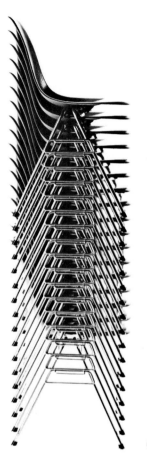

The most amusing of Eames' experiments with molded plastic is a one-piece chaise (called La Chaise) intended to have a factory price in 1948 of $27. The full-scale model (64, 65) is a stressed-skin shell which sandwiches a dense core of foamed, hard rubber between thin sheets of plastic. Variations in thickness provide strength where needed. The gestural quality of the shell is enhanced by its being perched on a pedestal combining no less than three different groups of elements. It is abstract sculpture in which one might sit, possibly quite comfortably.

**61** SIDE CHAIR. 1955.
Molded polyester; zinc-coated steel tube; rubber shockmounts; side hooks for stacking; nylon glides. 31¾" h.

**61**

**62**

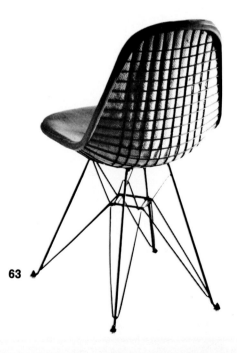

**63**

**62**   SIDE CHAIR. 1950.
     Molded polyester; wire; rubber shockmounts.
     31⅛″ h.

**63**   SIDE CHAIR. 1951.
     Formed black wire; padded tan leather. 32⅝″ h.

**64, 65**   CHAISE (full-scale model). 1948.
     Prototype for a stressed-skin shell: hard rubber
     foam between two layers of plastic. 32½″ h.

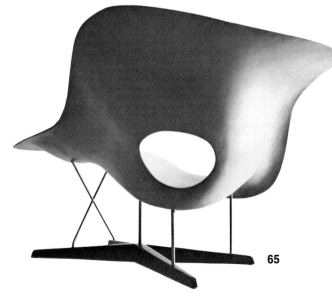

**65**

Most modern sofas are long, low, and heavy. Some designers have preferred to handle them as padded boxes resting squarely on the floor; some have preferred to perch them on light legs; many have preferred to avoid the problem altogether. (Of the other major modern furniture designers only Aalto and Breuer have produced sofas.)

A conspicuous difference in the Eames design is its high back, and the breaking of that element into two horizontal slabs which fold down for shipping. The design derives from a built-in sofa in the seating alcove of Eames' own house. There, however, a solid panel closed the space between the seat and the floor. The portable production version is carried on square-sectioned chrome-plated steel legs, with back supports of black-enameled steel (67). Perhaps because it originated as built-in furniture—an extension of his architecture—this design is uncharacteristically two-dimensional. Its configuration can be deduced from a drawing of the side elevation alone, unlike the compound curves of the molded wood chairs which cannot be "read" from drawings but must be seen in the round.

Meant primarily for office use and usually upholstered in vinyl, the design takes on more domestic connotations when covered in a textured cloth, which accentuates the modelling of its seat and back planes without making them look industrially polished.

Unlike most Eames designs, this one has not been modified to serve other standards of comfort. There is no version with arms, nor has Eames tried to develop the same configuration with softer padding. In contrast to the chrome legs, the armature-like black metal supports have an unexpectedly utilitarian look —unexpected since the sofa is designed to look well from all sides—and the different profiles used for the seat and back add another inconsistency. Yet the complete image manages to be at once svelte and Spartan; and it remains one of the few original solutions to a particularly difficult problem of furniture design.

66

67

**66, 67**   SOFA. 1954.
Chrome-plated and black-enameled steel frame;
black fabric over foam padding. 34½″ h. x 72″ w.
x 30½″ d.

**69**

Large seating units are most happily accommodated in modern interiors when they look architectural; that is, when they are geometric, box-like constructions, acting as massive foils to the lighter chairs which usually accompany them. Although modern chairs are as comfortable as those available to polite society in the 18th century, few modern furniture designers have been able to invent new forms for the kind of comfort provided only by well-padded cushions in generous sizes. Eames is the only designer to attempt a lounge chair which would surpass in comfort anything an English club can offer, and to achieve this comfort in formal terms consistent with his lighter, more casual designs.

Made of more parts than most Eames chairs, the lounge consists of three rosewood shells padded with leather cushions. These are filled with a mixture of down, latex foam, and grey duck feathers. Padded arm rests are encased in leather. The chair pivots on a five-pronged base of black aluminum with polished top surfaces; connectors supporting the two back shells are of the same material (68). An ottoman of similar design allows the chair to be used almost as a chaise.

The design of the rosewood shells is deceptive: curved across their width, they are flat on the longitudinal axis, and the combination of straight and curved lines is skillfully echoed in the metal fittings. Large enough to dominate any furniture grouping, but not too large to be arranged in groups themselves, the chair's rounded sculptural shape does not require fixed, formal placement.

**68** LOUNGE CHAIR AND OTTOMAN. 1956.
**69** Molded rosewood plywood; black leather cushions
**70** with foam, down, and feather filling; black and polished aluminum base; swivel (chair only). 33" h. Ottoman; 16" h.

**70**

71

72

73

Usually referred to as the "aluminum group", the chairs Eames introduced in 1958 use the thin, flat profile which first appeared in the sofa (66). But here the seat and back are made as one continuous plane slung between structural ribs of die-cast aluminum. Elaborately designed, the structure consists of six metal components in two different styles, with more structural detail concealed within the seat pad.

Perhaps the most interesting technical development is the seat itself, a "sandwich" consisting of front and back layers of fabric or vinyl, and an inner layer of vinyl-coated nylon fabric supporting a $\frac{1}{4}''$ thick layer of vinyl foam. This combination of materials is welded together through pressure and high frequency current. The welds occur at $1\frac{7}{8}''$ intervals, appearing as horizontal ribs or stripes on both sides of the pad (73, 74).

Cast in one piece, the side rib is modelled to form a bar and flange, and terminates at each end with a cylinder. Slipped into the flanges and secured in place with concealed brass nails, the seat pad wraps around the cylinders but is not itself stiffened across its top and bottom edges by any internal metal construction.

The supporting pedestal repeats the theme of flat bars and cylinders. It carries an intermediate stem of black steel, which in turn supports another die-cast aluminum element described as an "antler". This piece and a similar back brace are rounded shapes resembling bones. Although employing a design vocabulary different from that of the bar and cylinder, the scale of their curves and the similarity in finish avoids discord. The addition of arms, however, somewhat reduces coherence (71).

71, 73, 74    LOUNGE CHAIR. 1958.
              Polished die-cast aluminum; black painted tube;
              Naugahyde padded with vinyl foam. 35″ h.

72    SIDE CHAIR. 1958.
      Polished die-cast aluminum; black painted tube;
      Naugahyde padded with vinyl foam. 33½″ h.

**75, 76** LOUNGE CHAIR. 1958.
(Reclining high-back tilt-swivel chair.) Polished
die-cast aluminum; green fabric (or Naugahyde)
padded with vinyl foam. 39¾″ h.

75

76

**77**

**77, 78**  MULTIPLE SEATING. 1962.
Five-seat unit: polished aluminum; black steel
bars; padded vinyl. 33¾″ h.

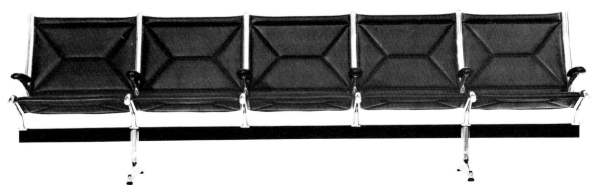

**78**

**79**

An interesting variation is the secretary's chair in which posture requirements produce a jaunty and elegant profile. This chair, like the others, is now available with a pedestal modelled in the same sculptural idiom as the antler and brace. A high-backed version of the lounge chair, almost duplicating the proportions of the sofa, incorporates a box-like housing for a tilt-swivel mechanism; this piece of hardware will be revised in a forthcoming version (75).

Tandem seating developed for use in airports combines a shaped arm and back with shaped seat and leg elements, connected to each other by flat steel bars coated black and looking like hardware acquired from another source. The interchangeable seat and back pads are, again, sandwiches of heat-sealed vinyl materials, the welds, however, being distributed to make a lozenge pattern similar to that used in oil cans or aluminum building panels to increase their strength (78).

All of the aluminum group chairs are startlingly light and comfortable. Their comfort is significantly increased by the addition of leather cushions in the group called "soft pad" chairs (80, 81). Similar in construction to their predecessors, these versions offer one seat and two or three back cushions filled with polyester foam and sewn to the nylon fabric support. The softer profile and surfaces relate well to the structural shapes, and the design regains consistency.

**80**

**79, 81**   LOUNGE CHAIR. 1969.
Polished die-cast aluminum; foam-padded tan leather cushions. 35¼″ h.

**80**   SIDE CHAIR. 1969.
Polished die-cast aluminum; foam-padded tan leather cushions. 33½″ h.

The long, narrow planes of this chaise are foreshadowed by some of the experimental plywood chairs of the 1940s (45), but its bone-like legs are part of a series of modifications of the aluminum group structural components (72, 73).

The metal frame carries a stretched, plasticized fabric, which in turn supports six leather cushions connected to each other with zippers. Additional loose cushions provide head or body support. The narrow dimensions and the lack of arms would seem to make repose almost mandatory; this is one of Eames' rare essays in form without function.

The padded leather swivel chair (82) is meant for executive suites but was originally developed for a semi-public reception area in a New York office building. Unusually comfortable, the chair has the interesting distinction of having been chosen by Bobby Fischer (and accepted by Boris Spassky) for use at the Reykjavík chess tournament. It also introduced a shaped leg that was subsequently adapted for several other chairs.

**82**

**83**

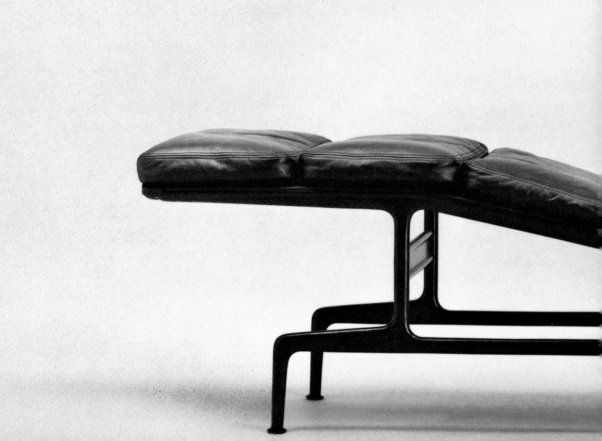

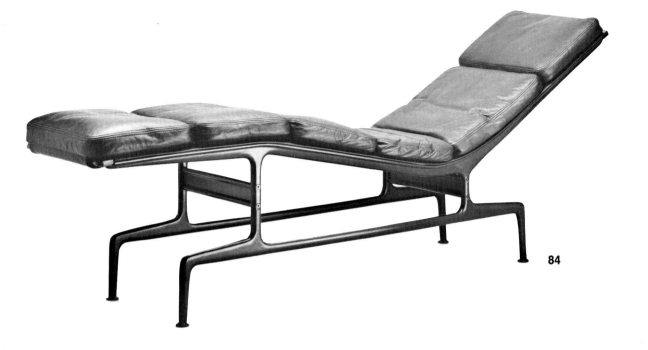

84

**82** LOUNGE CHAIR. 1960.
Polished aluminum; foam-padded tan leather cushions. 32½"-34½" h. (adjustable)

**83, 84** CHAISE. 1968.
Nylon-coated aluminum; foam-padded black leather cushions. 28¾" h.

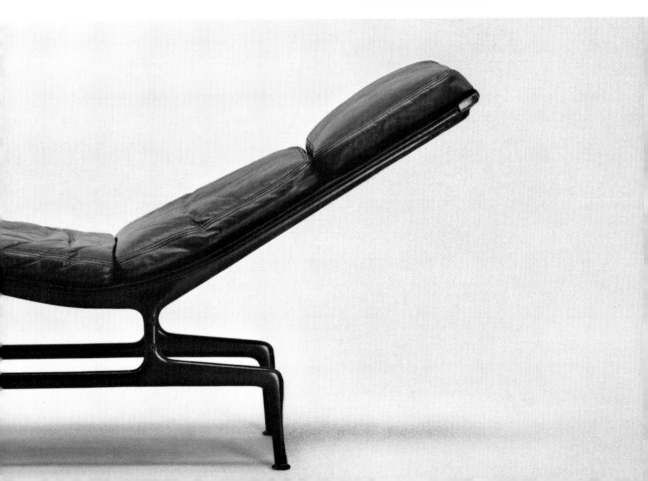

Of all the modifications Eames has made to his designs over a period of more than 30 years, by far the most consequential has been the addition of padded surfaces to chairs originally conceived as hard, thin planes of molded plywood or plastic. Padded surfaces (not illustrated) for the plastic shells of 1950 offer increased comfort but neither diminish nor enhance the design. But the padded version of the 1946 plywood dining chair is so substantially altered in its appearance as to be virtually a "new" design.

The major structural change is in materials: for this version seat and back shells are of plastic rather than wood, and each shell incorporates molded plastic housings containing metal units to which the legs and back support are bolted. An important visual change results from the technique of padding the plastic shells. Urethane foam is sandwiched between the shell and a "skin" of fabric or vinyl; the edges of the shells are then bound with a thick vinyl welt whose dimensions approximate those of the metal rod supports, thereby introducing a second set of lines complementing those of the legs. The combined modifications make lines visually more important than planes, although the new emphasis on soft surfaces is what occasioned the change.

**85, 86**  SIDE CHAIR. 1969.
Molded polyester; steel rods; padded Naugahyde with vinyl binding. 29½" h.

Although this chair might appear to be a padded version of the original 1950 plastic shell, its proportions differ from that design in two significant ways. The back support is 6" higher and makes up at least half the height of the entire shell; and the modelling of the inside back surface incorporates a reverse curve at its base, providing much firmer support. In addition, the chair's proportions are designed to include a loose seat cushion.

Technically, this chair is among Eames' most sophisticated and carefully studied productions. Its plastic shell receives a formed-in-place urethane foam padding, covered, like the upholstered side chair, by a vinyl or fabric skin. Dents in this material slowly disappear, the urethane having a "memory" for its original contours. A fabric or leather covering must be stitched; in vinyl the form is unbroken by this distracting detail, and every modulation of its curved surface is emphasized.

The padding varies in thickness from ¾" to 3", and its mass is suggested by the rolled edge of the shell (88). As in the upholstered side chair, a thick vinyl edge binding provides a strong outline, but in this case it relates only marginally to the linear quality of the base, which is the shaped aluminum design originally developed for the office lounge chair and later adapted for other models (82).

Sleek, polished, impeccably detailed, the molded and padded shell of this chair suggests the world of aviation. It also manages to be at once precise and voluptuous, and seems to convey as much of the mood or image of its day as the plywood furniture did in the 'forties.

**87**

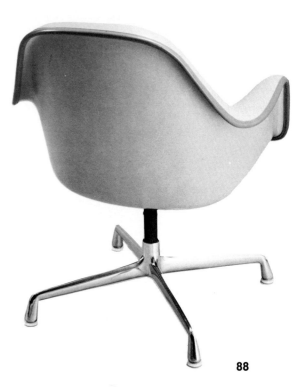

**88**

**87, 88, 89** ARMCHAIR. 1971.
Molded polyester; aluminum base; padded Naugahyde with vinyl binding; loose cushion. 32" h.

*Photographers' credits:* All photos by Stan Ries except as follows: Alfred Auerbach Associates, 59; George Barrows, 17-20, 63; Charles Eames, 28-9, 34, 41-2, 44-5, 47, 49, 55, 58, 61-2, 77-8; Samuel Gottscho, 1; Herman Miller Inc., 27; Museum of Modern Art, 15, 21, 48; Herbert Matter, 37; Julius Shulman, 56-7; Soichi Sunami, 2-14, 31-3, 35-6, 39, 43. Research: Mary Jane Lightbown.

The Museum acknowledges with gratitude the generous assistance of Charles and Ray Eames in the preparation of this catalog and the exhibition it accompanies. We are also grateful to Herman Miller Inc. for their many gifts to the Design Collection; and to Robert Blaich and John Buglisi for assistance in research and photography.

# CATALOG

The check list includes all works by Charles Eames in the Museum's Design Collection. Illustration numbers are given in the margin. Details of construction refer to the example in the Collection; earlier or later production may differ. The date accompanying each entry indicates when the object was first manufactured; some examples in the Collection are current production. Accession numbers, given in parentheses, do not necessarily correspond to dates of design or manufacture. The letters SC indicate Study Collection.

## SIDE CHAIRS

**24**
**53** DINING CHAIR. 1946. (553.53; 80.48)
Molded walnut (also ash) plywood; steel rod; rubber shockmounts; rubber and metal glides. 29½″ h. x 20½″ w. x 21½″ d.
Gift of the manufacturer: Herman Miller Inc.

**40** DINING CHAIR. 1946. (70.46)
Molded and bent birch plywood; rubber shockmounts. 29½″ h. x 19″ w. x 21½″ d.
Gift of the manufacturer: Evans Products Co.

**62** SIDE CHAIR. 1950. (SC 100.73)
Yellow molded polyester reinforced with glass fibers; wire struts; rubber shockmounts; metal glides. 31⅛″ h. x 18½″ w. x 22″ d.
Manufacturer: Herman Miller Inc.
Gift of Charles Eames.

**63** SIDE CHAIR. 1951. (217.53)
Formed black wire; padded tan leather; metal glides. 32⅝″ h. x 18⅞″ w. x 20⅞″ d.
Gift of the manufacturer: Herman Miller Inc.

SIDE CHAIR. 1951. (218.53)
Formed wire; wood legs; beige tweed fabric pads; swivel mount. 32¼″ h. x 19″ w. x 20½″ d.
Gift of the manufacturer: Herman Miller Inc.

**61** SIDE CHAIR, Stacking. 1955. (SC 101.73)
Red molded polyester reinforced with glass fibers; zinc-coated steel tube; rubber shockmounts; side hooks for stacking; nylon glides. 31¾″ h. x 23½″ w. x 21½″ d.
Gift of the manufacturer: Herman Miller Inc.

**72** SIDE CHAIR. 1958. (153.73)
Polished die cast aluminum; black painted tube; charcoal Naugahyde padded with vinyl foam; nylon glides. 33½″ h. x 21″ w. x 22½″ d.
Gift of the manufacturer: Herman Miller Inc.

**80** SIDE CHAIR. 1969. (154.73)
Polished die cast aluminum; black painted tube; tan leather cushions with polyester foam padding; nylon glides. 33½″ h. x 21″ w. x 22½″ d.
Gift of the manufacturer: Herman Miller Inc.

**85** SIDE CHAIR. 1969. (155.73)
Black molded polyester reinforced with glass fibers; chrome-plated steel rod; imbedded T-nut studs; off-white Naugahyde with polyurethane foam padding; black vinyl edge binding; nylon glides. 29½″ h. x 19½″ w. x 21½″ d.
Gift of the manufacturer: Herman Miller Inc.

**38** LOW SIDE CHAIR. 1946. (64.46)
Molded and bent birch plywood; tan padded leather laminated to wood; rubber shockmounts. 25½″ h. x 22½″ w. x 25¼″ d.
Gift of the manufacturer: Evans Products Co.

**39** LOW SIDE CHAIR. 1946. (SC 102.73)
Molded and bent ash plywood; rubber shockmounts. 25¾″ h. x 22¼″ w. x 25″ d. Gift of Eugene Eppinger.
Manufacturer: Evans Products Co.

**29** LOW SIDE CHAIR. 1946. (156.73)
Molded walnut plywood; chrome-plated steel rod; rubber shockmounts; nylon glides. 27⅜″ h. x 22¼″ w. x 25⅜″ d.
Gift of the manufacturer: Herman Miller Inc.

SIDE CHAIR. 1940. With Eero Saarinen. (842.42)
Molded plywood; fabric; sponge rubber padding. 33″ h. x 18″ w. x 21½″ d.
Manufacturer: Haskelite Mfg. Corp. and Heywood-Wakefield Co. Purchase. First prize for seating, "Organic Design in Home Furnishings" competition, MOMA. 1941.

**33** SIDE CHAIR, Three-legged. c. 1944. (67.46)
Molded plywood stained red; metal rod; single back leg of doubled rod; rubber shockmounts; rubber glides. 29½″ h. x 19″ w. x 22¼″ d.
Gift of the manufacturer: Evans Products Co.

SIDE CHAIR, Three-legged. c. 1944. (66.46)
Molded plywood stained black; metal rod lacquered black; rubber shockmounts; rubber glides. 30″ h. x 19″ w. x 22½″ d.
Gift of the manufacturer: Evans Products Co.

**34** SIDE CHAIR, Three-legged. c. 1944. (65.46)
Molded canaletta plywood; metal rod lacquered black; rubber shockmounts; rubber glides. 29¾″ h. x 19″ w. x 20″ d.
Gift of the manufacturer: Evans Products Co.

**35** SIDE CHAIR, Tilt-back. c. 1944. (69.46)
Molded plywood; single and double metal rods; rubber shockmounts; rubber glides. 25¾″ h. x 20″ w. x 29″ d.
Gift of the manufacturer: Evans Products Co.

**36** SIDE CHAIR, Tilt-back. c. 1944. (68.46)
Molded walnut plywood; steel bars and rods lacquered black; rubber shockmounts; rubber glides. 26″ h. x 21½″ w. x 28½″ d.
Gift of the manufacturer: Evans Products Co.

SIDE CHAIR (full-scale model). 1948. With University of California Team. (SC 31.50)
Neoprene-coated aluminum shell, painted yellow; aluminum pedestal. 30″ h. x 17¾″ w. x 20½″ d.
Co-winner of second prize for seating, International Competition for Low-Cost Furniture, MOMA. 1948.

SIDE CHAIR (full-scale model). 1948. With University of California Team. (SC 32.50)
Neoprene-coated aluminum shell, painted black; wood legs. 31″ h. x 17¾″ w. x 20″ d.
Co-winner of second prize for seating, International Competition for Low-Cost Furniture, MOMA. 1948.

## ARMCHAIRS

**60** ARMCHAIR. 1950. (448.56)
White molded polyester reinforced with glass fibers; metal tube; rubber shockmounts; plastic glides. 31¼″ h. x 24⅞″ w. x 23½″ d.
Manufacturer: Herman Miller Inc.
Gift of Elaine Lustig.

ARMCHAIR. 1950. (267.58)
White molded polyester reinforced with glass fibers; wire struts; rubber shockmounts; plastic glides. 30¼″ h. x 25″ w. x 23¾″ d.
Gift of the manufacturer: Herman Miller Inc.

**59** ARMCHAIR, Rocker. 1950. (349.50)
Gray molded polyester reinforced with glass fibers; wire; birch runners; rubber shockmounts. 26¾″ h. x 25″ w. x 26⅝″ d.
Gift of the manufacturer: Herman Miller Inc.

**58** LOW ARMCHAIR. 1950. (350.50)
Beige molded polyester reinforced with glass fibers; wire cage; rubber shockmounts. 23″ h. x 24¾″ w. x 24½″ d.
Gift of the manufacturer: Herman Miller Inc.

ARMCHAIR (full-scale model). 1948. With University of California Team. (SC 33.50)
Neoprene-coated aluminum shell, painted gray; metal rod. 29″ h. x 27½″ w. x 24¼″ d.
Co-winner of second prize for seating, International Competition for Low-Cost Furniture, MOMA. 1948.

ARMCHAIR, Rocker (full-scale model). 1948. With University of California Team. (SC 34.50)
Neoprene-coated aluminum shell, painted brown; metal rod; wood runners. 28½″ h. x 27¾″ w. x 27⅝″ d.
Co-winner of second prize for seating, International Competition for Low-Cost Furniture, MOMA. 1948.

**51** ARMCHAIR. 1971. (157.73)
**87** Black molded polyester reinforced with glass fibers; polished aluminum base; black painted tube; beige Naugahyde with urethane foam padding; black vinyl edge binding; loose hopsack cushion; swivel mechanism; nylon glides. 32″ h. x 26″ w. x 28″d.
Gift of the manufacturer: Herman Miller Inc.

## LOUNGE CHAIRS

**54** LOUNGE CHAIR and OTTOMAN. 1956. (336.60 a-b)
**69** Molded rosewood plywood; black leather cushions with latex foam, feathers and down filling; flexible aluminum connectors; black and aluminum swivel base; rubber shockmounts; metal glides. 33″ h. x 33¾″ w. x 33″ d.
*Ottoman.* Materials same as above. 16″ h. x 26″ w. x 21″ d.
Gift of the manufacturer: Herman Miller Inc.

**71** LOUNGE CHAIR. 1958. (SC 103.73)
Polished die cast aluminum frame and arms; black painted tube; charcoal Naugahyde padded with vinyl foam; nylon glides. 34½″ h. x 25½″ w. x 27¼″ d.
Gift of the manufacturer: Herman Miller Inc.

**50** LOUNGE CHAIR. 1958. (148.58)
**73** Polished die cast aluminum; black painted tube; charcoal Naugahyde padded with vinyl foam; nylon glides. 35″ h. x 22″ w. x 27″ d.
Gift of the manufacturer: Herman Miller Inc.

**75** LOUNGE CHAIR. 1958. (SC 104.73 a-b)
Polished die cast aluminum; green fabric padded with vinyl foam; steel tilt/swivel mechanism; nylon glides. 39¾″ h. x 23″ w. x 30″ d.
*Ottoman.* Materials same as above. 18″ h. x 21½″ w. x 21⅛″ d.
Gift of the manufacturer: Herman Miller Inc.

**79** LOUNGE CHAIR. 1969. (SC 105.73)
Polished die cast aluminum frame and arms; tan leather cushions with polyester foam padding; nylon glides. 35¼″ h. x 25½″ w. x 27¼″ d.
Gift of the manufacturer: Herman Miller Inc.

**81** LOUNGE CHAIR. 1969. (158.73)
Polished die cast aluminum; tan leather cushions with polyester foam padding; nylon glides. 35¼″ h. x 24½″ w. x 27¼″ d.
Gift of the manufacturer: Herman Miller Inc.

**82** LOUNGE CHAIR. 1960. (SC 109.73)
Polished aluminum frame and arms; tan leather cushions and arm rests with foam padding; steel tilt/swivel mechanism; adjustable base; nylon glides. 32½″-34½″ h. x 26½″ w. x 27″ d.
Gift of the manufacturer: Herman Miller Inc.

**83** CHAISE. 1968. (SC 110.73)
Eggplant nylon-coated aluminum frame; stretched plasticized fabric sheet supports six black leather cushions connected by zippers; polyester foam padding. 28¾″ h. x 75″ w. x 17½″ d.
Gift of the manufacturer: Herman Miller Inc.

LOUNGE CHAIR. 1940. With Eero Saarinen. (840.42)
Molded plywood; fabric; sponge rubber padding. 33″ h. x 29½″ w. x 26″ d. Manufacturer: Haskelite Mfg. Corp. and Heywood-Wakefield Co. Purchase. First prize for seating, "Organic Design in Home Furnishings" competition, MOMA. 1941.

LOUNGE CHAIR. 1940. With Eero Saarinen. (841.42)
Molded plywood; fabric; sponge rubber padding. 42½″ h. x 32¾″ w. x 31¾″ d. Manufacturer: Haskelite Mfg. Corp. and Heywood-Wakefield Co. Purchase. First prize for seating, "Organic Design in Home Furnishings" competition, MOMA. 1941.

**44** LOUNGE CHAIR, Tilt-back. c. 1944. (160.73)
Molded plywood with metal rod. 28″ h. x 30⅛″ w. x 31″ d.
Gift of Charles Eames.

**64** CHAISE (full-scale model). 1948. (SC 106.73)
Prototype for a stressed-skin shell: hard rubber foam between two layers of plastic, painted gray; wood and metal rod base. 32½″ h. x 59″ w. x 34¼″ d.
Gift of Charles Eames.

## MULTIPLE SEATING

**52** SOFA. 1954. (450.56)
**66** Black-enameled steel frame; chrome-plated steel legs; interlinked flat steel springs; black fabric with foam padded seat and back; stainless steel glides. 34½″ h. x 72″ w. x 30½″ d.
Gift of the manufacturer: Herman Miller Inc.

**77 MULTIPLE SEATING. 1962 (SC 107.73)**
Five-seat unit: individual seat and back cushions suspended between polished aluminum frames secured to a continuous black epoxy-finished steel T-beam; steel connector bar; interchangeable black vinyl pads; vinyl foam padding; padded arm rests; plastic glides. 33¾" h. x 117¼" w. x 28" d.
Gift of the manufacturer: Herman Miller Inc.

## TABLES

**37 COFFEE TABLE. 1946. (159.73)**
Molded plywood circular tray top; three metal legs; shockmounts; metal glides. 15¾" h. x 34¼" dia.
Manufacturer: Evans Products Co.
Gift of Charles Eames.

**49 FOLDING DINING TABLE. 1947. (SC 108.73)**
White plastic top on wood; folding metal legs. 28⅞" h. x 33⅞" w. x 53⅞" l.
Gift of the manufacturer: Herman Miller Inc.

## STORAGE

**1 STORAGE CABINETS. 1940. With Eero Saarinen. (853-860.42)**
Eight wood cabinets, Honduras mahogany veneer; all 18" or 36" wide; 22" high and 18" deep; with varying arrangements of drawers and shelves; designed to rest on 13" high benches.
Manufacturer: Red Lion Table Co. Purchase. First prize, Living Room Furniture, "Organic Design in Home Furnishings" competition, MOMA. 1941.

**1 BENCHES. 1940. With Eero Saarinen. (850-852.42)**
Three wood benches, Honduras mahogany veneer; 13" high and 18" deep; lengths are 36", 54" and 72"; holding two, three and four cabinets (see above).
Manufacturer: Red Lion Table Co. Purchase. First prize, Living Room Furniture, "Organic Design in Home Furnishings" competition, MOMA. 1941.

## MISCELLANEOUS

**BENCH. 1946. (63.46)**
Birch top; demountable molded plywood legs. 12" h. x 16" w. x 54½" l.
Gift of the manufacturer: Evans Products Co.

**46 FOLDING SCREEN. 1946. (79.48)**
Molded ash plywood in 9½" sections; canvas joints. 68" h. x 60" l.
Manufacturer: Evans Products Co.
Gift of Herman Miller Inc.

**16 LEG SPLINT. 1942. (SC 24.50)**
Molded plywood. 4¾" h. x 7¾" w. x 41½" l.
Manufacturer: Evans Products Co.
Gift of Charles Eames.

**CHILD'S CHAIR. c. 1944. (82.48)**
Molded plywood stained red. 14½" h. x 14½" w. x 11" d.
Manufacturer: Evans Products Co.
Gift of Herman Miller Inc.

## DRAWINGS

**3-10 COMPETITION DRAWINGS. 1940. With Eero Saarinen. (861-870.42)**
Ten first prize designs submitted for "Organic Design in Home Furnishings" competition, MOMA. 1941. Side chair; easy chair; conversation chair; relaxation chair; sofa unit; lounging shape; coffee table; cabinet units; radio-record player-bar unit. Colored pencil, wood veneer and paper cut-outs on white poster board. 20" x 30".

**COMPETITION DRAWINGS. 1948. With University of California Team. (SC 35-43.50)**
Seven panels, co-winner second prize for seating, International Competition for Low-Cost Furniture, MOMA. 1948. Assorted designs for molded shell seating. Photographs and ink drawings on white poster board. 20" x 30".
By Charles Eames alone: two panels, design for plastic chaise in stressed-skin construction.

09 246